To Newfoundland

To Newfoundland

POEMS BY

Caroline Knox

The University of Georgia Press

ATHENS AND LONDON

© 1989 by Caroline Knox
Published by the University of Georgia Press
Athens, Georgia 30602
All rights reserved
Designed by Betty McDaniel
Set in Sabon with Zapf Chancery
The paper in this book meets the guidelines for
permanence and durability of the Committee on
Production Guidelines for Book Longevity of the
Council on Library Resources.

Printed in the United States of America

93 92 91 90 89   5 4 3 2 1

Library of Congress Cataloging in Publication Data

Knox, Caroline.
To Newfoundland.

(Contemporary poetry series)
I. Title.   II. Series: Contemporary poetry series
(University of Georgia Press)
PS3561.N686T6   1989   811'.54   88-26082
ISBN 0-8203-1114-6 (alk. paper)
ISBN 0-8203-1115-4 (pbk. : alk. paper)

British Library Cataloging in Publication Data available

Acknowledgments

The author is extremely grateful to the National Endowment for the Arts, a federal agency, and to the Ingram Merrill Foundation for support while this book was being written.

The New Republic: "The Stone Calendar," "Log of the *Snow Star*."
Shenandoah: "Background," "Off Gems Bund," "To Newfoundland," "The Heart."
Ploughshares: "Pantoum du chat."
New Virginia Review: "A Song for St. Cecilia's Day."
The Red Fox Review: "Beach Poem."
The Massachusetts Review: "Lizzie Borden Through Art and Literature."
The Anglican Theological Review: "Souvenir de Roc-Amadour," "Sestina for Bishop Seabury," "Becoming Girl Scouts."
Chiaroscuro: "Dean and Later Bishop," "Gerhard Thorpe, Male Nurse," "The Farley Family."
The Apalachee Quarterly: "Teeth," "Freudian Shoes," "Exploring Unknown Territory."
Light Year: "The Urn," "Give Me an A."
New American Writing: "Movement Along the Frieze."
Cream City Review: "Emblem Poem: Scallop Shell."
"Movement Along the Frieze" also appeared in *Best Poetry of 1988,* ed. John Ashbery (New York: Scribners, 1988).
"The True Rag" (a stanza of "The Farley Family") appeared in another form in the *Cream City Review* and in the *Anglican Theological Review.*

Contents

To Newfoundland

The Stone Calendar

The personnel of January are standing
stones with two traditional faces.

Faces that are the lard and cinders
of February. I was watching them there

where the moon of March lit them
and behold they said they were cold

yet not so cold in April as
previously. Further, there were pleasant

side-effects such as the expected May flowers
which put some slight blush there on them

which fulminated, inasmuch as it became
June. So they mopped their brows

in July too. Pah! in August with
quadrants of leafy faces. Only

in September they with tempered
relief rest in tawny shade, with

dolor too for the October nasty
winds and November more follow.

So there they ever are almost back where they
began in December looking at the chilly prospect.

Beach Poem

This poem proceeds matter-of-factly up from the basis
of particulars, hidden element, deliberate
premises of sandpipers' amusing feet, occupationally
cold, but they like it like that, they don't mind a bit

and this here bird digresses from other patterers
as the current stanza diverges if only slightly
in the expensive lenses of uncomfortable muffled birdwatchers
luminous girder-colored lumps on sticks

The streets of the New World are paved with broken *gasp*
glass the shards of the Industrial Revolution
but naturally mellowed out by constant whacking and sifting

Hence will you not walk on the topos of previous perishing
literary remarks about mortality and mutability?
on this moratorium more or less of stone and water?
the combers are hyper and if you'll forgive me navy blue

and hollow and bright. Leaving weirdo interesting
striped horizontal grittings in the somewhat severe
arenaria groenlandica. This last upholds a kind of compact
with the vegetable; the mineral I've sufficiently touched on

Becoming Girl Scouts

I am afraid we will fly up
flap up we are so full of worms
and our skins aren't any longer pink
or sticky but all wings. I'm afraid we will—
we're going higher; and we were so recently
doing these same muscular things
on the nice grass and the brown tree.

My, the ingenuous broad bulk of the leader
shifts on her chair on the stage, and we'd better
zoom over to the public rite which is now beginning.
My goodness, will I land in her lap?
Nope, she's standing, she's reading the lines that right now
are turning us into new creatures!   new green birds!
Can you beat that, you guys—
down there, that terrible onerous regeneration of feathers!

Background
A Poem in Envy of Baudelaire

I want a canvas boudoir pinked with runes
where I can belt out mannerist broadsides evincing me
at sea in the sky, so my neighbors will consist of bells
and the wind will blow their religious bongs in my dreams.
I will thus note the alfresco phenomena of Victorian
optimism's urban obelisk and cylinder or whatever
with my mopish chin in my hands.
                             For what I ask you
could possibly be more divine that the cocktail hour's
four nightlights: Venus, but also my gooseneck lamp,
the Hudson River School of the Aurora Borealis
up and down the firmament. Fourth, the adulated moon's
    dispatch
of pale enchantment. Ditto spring summer fall
and monochromatic winter as who should know. I'll blanket
myself in textiles thank you and muffle
in the spongecake monoliths of Las Percales.
At which point I'll dream all the pedagogic baggage
of Western Civ: provincial ballparks, provisionally
morphic blue horizons at length, and smoochings,
symbolic birds sounding off around the clock and other
    earmarks
of the leftovers of the bombast and piffle of Courtly Love.
Thus Prince in all sorts of positive and negative and actually
neutral nature experiences or at least impressions of same
it's business as usual. Disguised, the storm will roar
and the image I'm getting is highly well maybe this isn't
what you talk about but ecstatic and closely allied to
    determining
some sort of climate of stability from burning issues if you take
    me.

Pantoum du chat

Charles and I go out together
in his boat, which is a cat-
amaran, in the burnishing weather,
elated, so it's not surprising that

in his boat, which is a cat
at top speed among cats, this poem begins.
Elated, so it's not surprising that
we sing "Speed Bonnie Boat" to the winds.

At top speed among cats, this poem begins
making me seasick. "This malady," says Charles, "will become,
as we sing 'Speed Bonnie Boat' to the winds,
as naught," preventing them from

making me seasick. "This malady," says Charles, "will become
the narrative wave of the future, the wave of metaphor,
the wave of Narragansett Bay, of foam.
All the cliché for cats: liquid, longueur, languor,

the narrative wave. Of the future: the wave of metaphor,
I say, will be transfigured by the cat.
All the cliché for cats: liquid, longueur, languor,
as among poems this wave begins that

I say will be transfigured by the cat
as the cat leaps, you know, in timely weather.
All this of course in a Catamaran Voice, the times that
Charles and I go out together.

Give Me an A

Give me an A
A capital
as Dürer made A and D his own

A calls the other letters
in all the languages
come here   come here
Q peculiar   necessary U
roll me over R and steadfast I
says A

and cheered or grumbling
bumping up against each other
getting out of line becoming words
and lining up they're characters

Souvenir de Roc-Amadour

Clydesdales with feet like plungers exhaust themselves
long before they reach the view-encrusted decoupage
of your belled summits, turfless town, whence a tumble
necessarily results in the valleys of geology.
Biographed in *The Gentle Giants,* an expensive book,
the best stompers in St. Louis are no match for you.
But your winding mountain path where the valiant Renault
lies fallow would be unsuitable even for Arabian
aristocratic streakers. I see them puzzled by your steeps,
the dear bloods, digging out for the respite of the Massif
    Central.

Hunting's a practice that brooks no acrophobia,
a negative for the crag, oh hamlet small.
A pity, too, since hunting's so medieval,
in genesis, at least, and what one wears.
So the chase would enhance the press and crush of the pilgrim
giving a wide berth to gentians and edelweiss, stalking
eyes front to the peaked village above in its pendulous beauty!
And what if he saw—marvelous—the squire and his lady
riding to hounds, and saw the hounds, too, barreling
through tiny pinnacled cobblestone streets! through ancient
    gutters!

And there of course the merry Alp-like air drunkens
the pilgrim who has broached his destination. Oxygen
if he knows it is at a premium in an audible yodel;
were he a scientist he could conduct experiments,
ballooning among them, to give a fresh perspective.
Burgesses and churchwardens, so far from being alarmed
at notoriety incurred by dirigibles or *l'affichage céleste,*

rather encourage it as productive to the jurisdiction
of their bailiwick, and salubrious to humankind.
Or he might be a woman, Mademoiselle from Armentières.

But for this purpose he is not. Who is the gnarled crosspatch
who would make the pilgrim forego his times, bucolics,
georgics and eclogues (metamorphic or igneous
or sedimentary all) and rolls in the hay?
Too soon, too sudden he is caught in the Southwest
Midlands, in England, in Leeds even, at factory toil,
wed to a plump fiction, deviled by gray-faced creditors,
or Elkhart, Indiana, at the manufacture of not-very-good
band instruments. Unto his dimpled progeny, then,
by the grate at evening, oh town, he reconstructs you in undying
    song.

Railroads and Newspapers

As we rode the Chicago Milwaukee St. Paul and Pacific
Railroad we read the paper—the *Chicago Sun-Times* and the
   Minneapolis Tribune,
recalling that on the New York New Haven and Hartford of
   blessed memory it used to be terrific

to read the *New Haven Register,* the *Hartford Courant,* and the
   Times, prolific
as we were. Then we rode the Chesapeake and Ohio and pretty
   soon
out the window we saw some rolling stock from the Chicago
   Milwaukee St. Paul and Pacific.

During this leg of what turned out to be a trip we read the
   Cleveland Plain Dealer and the *Detroit Free Press*—the
   funnies, to be specific.
Then we rode the tiny, arcanely distinguished Detroit and
   Mackinac Railroad and the moon
rose over the Lower Forty-Eight, sentimental and honorific.

If Ic-
arus had ridden the rails in his hybristic noon,
the Chicago Milwaukee St. Paul and Pacific

Railroad would have been his dish of tea. Diffic-
ult to imagine. Under the obituary page of the *New Orleans
   Times-Picayune*
we slept editorially, such thoughts being soporific,

yet at which point the locomotive up ahead exploded in a fiery
   blue crash and we were all killed instantly (and signific-

ant people promptly read about it in the *Chicago Sun-Times*
and the *Minneapolis Tribune*)
on the Chicago Milwaukee St. Paul and Pacific
Railroad, a fur piece from the late New York New Haven and
Hartford. What a wonderful outfit *that* was. Wasn't it terrific.

A Song for St. Cecilia's Day 1987

Cecilia will always play
the organ
with her galoshes on
so she
can
hit more notes that way.
Laryngitis is her
nemesis.
Stuffed under her misericorde is a
scrumptious roman à clef
invoking Bliss Carman and Blossom Dearie
to read on breaks during this frequent ad-hoc get-together.

Frank's Drum Shop off Adams
Street in the Loop supplies
the Zildjian cymbals and the Ludwig drums
for the occasion. The shaggy drummer cries,
"Today
we had an outdoor
Chem class. You can have more
explosions that way."

Then beer and wine and Tab and Coke
(innocuous, low-octane grog) and scads of food
which no one would
show up without, appear:
kielbasa and onions
roasted the way they are
in the streets of Warsaw on St. Cecilia's Day.
Hot mushrooms stuffed with themselves and scallions,
somebody's mysterious, rich standby—tortellin

i and lima bean
salad with hearts of artichoke.
This actually tastes really good.

The trumpeter is an introvert whose might and ardor
Chris
topher Hogwood's dis
tinguished biography of Handel touches on, this
"singular idea or *Affekt*"
in the candid blasts and blore
of said trumpeter's snaky cuspidor.

"I'm certainly glad I never took up the
violin," said a
cellist invented by John
Ashbery and James Schuyler in *A Nest of Ninnies*.
"It's so confusing
not to have something
to lean on."
This remark might just
have been made by the cellist of record in his slump
of severe
orthopedic difficulties,
which don't somehow interfere
with the timing
of the august,
deliberate indecisiveness
of his gorgeous, triumph
alistic lows.

The two fiddlers are his buddies
and roomies.
Not much is known about either one
by anybody, because they say little and that in unison,
believing

that everything
is pretty OK and great
and so are in a position to concentrate.

All scowling five males are of course spaced out
on the girl flutist
whose sufficient blond ponytail shines
beyond the silver flute,
but only one of them is sleeping
with her—it's the drummer. They
haven't told anybody about it. Weeping
seeds of little tears, sighs for the recent curve of
the drummer's sweaty back, if we only knew,
all for love
(toward the others she's a Platonist);
but off goes the flute narrative now concerning divers pearls
of dryads, Naiads, and such-
like girls
and in triads, huge
and various Deist
ically oriented Papist
subterfuge,
much
as "care
less and dar
ing" Miss Mar
gar
et Bryant calls Dryden's stan
zas in the Eleventh Edition (1911) of the Encyclopedia
Britan
nica.

Music, as Auden not too long
ago observed, does not smell,

while John Russell
in the *Times* more recently said:
"Cherubim
open their mouths wide in compulsory song,"
by way of doxology,
and we should hark to him
as well.
Artful Cecilia clomps the sacred premises,
and all the whiffling bellows to produce the notes is made
from old Electroluxes in a Rube
Goldberg arrangement. The whole thing gets taped and shown
on the tube.

Emblem Poem: Scallop Shell

Calico Scallop

Je voudrais les coquilles Saint-Jacques, s'il vous plaît

There's supposed to be a picture of the object
at the top of the emblem poem, so here it is:
the scallop shell, its reaches cut in copper
(as otherwise poured in sterling for baptism):
a convenient and corded shape, a grainy or pinto
bisque of a finish, a sunburst which is printed
muted and speckled, to crackle on the shingle;
and under the picture there's supposed to be
(according to *English Emblem Books,* by Rosemary
Freeman) a motto in a foreign language,
as suits the poet. So this is what I said
to the waiter when Michael and I were at Mystic:
May I please have some *coquilles Saint-Jacques?*
How will the gentle reader figure, though,
at this point in the poem, where there's meant to be
an application of all the foregoing matter
that's ethically and esthetically good for you?
Not everyone gets to go to Santiago
de Campostela, or wants to, but pilgrims
of any stripe bear the scallop badge
to this holy land or that one, depending.
And look, my lines to you were stamped with it,
an emblem of an emblem of grace.

Lady Godiva

Dear Leofric,

I'm at Hadrian's Wall. This was our lunch today: (1) Banbury
Tarts. (2) Scones in consistency like the Stone of the same name.
(3) Stilton Cheese, in profusion. (4) Metheglin. The Wall is
falling down in places, but there's agitation to fix it from the
most boring lot of antiquarians, always talking about their
long-gone kinship with Anchises, e.g. One lardy lady says she
knows a man who has met someone who has read the Fall of
Troy in a book. Then there are some of them arguing that the
whole thing should be torn *down.* Or left as a "ruin." Or
restored to what nobody even knows whether it looked like or
not.

Now here's how things are at the monastery. Everything
outdoors looks *grand,* all picked up and brushed and combed
from last year; the thrips look completely gone. A sausage of a
dog, who lives handsomely off the kitchen, met me; his name is
Mr. Glossy-Coat-by-Reason-of-Fish-Oil. This morning in the
kitchen garden the brother says to me: *dixit:* Wouldn't it be
great if watercress grew out of the tops of radishes? and parsley
out of the tops of carrots? then we'd hardly need anything else
to eat, would we? *Et ego autem:* Well, yes, it would be great.
Similarly, upstairs in the library this joke is (often) made:
"Hand me over the vichyssoise—I mean the library paste." (The
joke also works in reverse at the dinner table.) *Entre nous,*
dearest, they're all still hanging at the pap to a degree,
confusing a) God with Sex, and b) the Self with the Other. To a
degree. Refectory reading matter: at noon, Barphomedes of
Pukos; at night, Bugbites.

Chroniclers are beginning to abound, more and more
unreliable. Some are disaffected millenarists. They have all

cleverly capitalized on the Coventry Carol, so that pilgrims visit and buy their semidelicious monastery-made treats, and the whole place prospers. Far and near our monks are known as the Lullay Brothers, and the shrine as Little-Tiny-Child. There are indecent versions of the holy text, by the way, which I hope to copy. The monks are very proud of the library treasures, such as an autographed picture of the Danelaw (well, that's what they *say*), and the Vermicelli Book, and also the *Cartularia Saxonica,* which could be used for pressing to death if wanted. What do these religious know about a Little Tiny Child.

But the world shouldn't rely on your occasional oddball earl's wife to reduce taxes and redistribute responsibility. Some of the nobles themselves should go to see the monarch and should sit her or him down under a tree. And politely force her or him to give them power, a certain appropriate amount of power. A council theory and then make it work. They should do that sometime. In this vein of order, I am deeply bothered that dear Aelfgar, wild and free, seems to have allied himself with Gryffydd ap Llewellyn and his druids and for all I know a host of corgis. The system of taxation is very nice indeed for the king. But it is cumbrous, overelaborate, and inequitable for the people. You can believe that as soon as my ride was finished I went and put on my cosy and comfortable and simple garments in token of what I hope results: better lives for the people. We're all sure we don't know what will happen.

And in the vein of power, last night's (twenty-year-old) story-poem in resonant (if nasal) Norman couplets. It went something like this, although I do not reproduce the Norman. King Canute the Great, the pious extortionist whom as you know you may thank for your earldom, personified the ocean and then spoke to it, as one in a series of memorable (if dotty) acts. With great vigor of authority, and having his sedan chair on the very edge of the sea, Canute said to the rising tide, "You are in my sway; and the earth in which I sit is mine: nor can the earth resist my command. Therefore I order you not to rise onto my land, nor to presume to wet either the garments or the legs of your overlord!" The sea, spreading as it will, rose up irreverently over the feet and then the legs of the king. Recoiling, Canute very gracefully modulated into the expected set piece *de contemptu mundi* and the Fall of Princes: "Let all the inhabitants of the world know how empty and trivial," and so forth. A fine poem, fine delivery. And Canute *on dit* was excelled as an administrator only by Alfred.

This whole tax procedure could be done federally, not just in Coventry. I don't mean ladies riding around naked with their teeth chattering, etc.; but the monarch could make a small tax for the thrall and a large tax for the Sieur de Pelf. De Pelf wouldn't miss it. This could be a graduated tax. Another move is to get rid of the disgusting lotteries. Would you please think about tax. I'm going on the Wall this afternoon with the huckleberry pickers. And with the Society for the Preservation of the Past. They're going to find Aeneas's old thongs. They don't realize that things *weren't* old then.

We need to say this together when I get back. I was the peace-weaver without a stitch on. There shouldn't be any taxation without representation, but there is, all over the *wapentake*. If there *was* a man looking through the shutters, he was and is a loathesome curd. May the *Cartularia Saxonica* fall on him. But to you: HUGS, physical, spiritual, and mental, which should cover everything. This is one of the ironies. If I put my physical arms tight around you, I'm hugging the rest, too.

Godiva

Freudian Shoes

Freudian shoes, the puddings of orthopedic flight
marginally confining doves of feet which might actually be a
    female Everyman's,
but with this sublime caveat: vermilion please not to say alizarin
crimson flame-stitch and water-silk uppers
with the atavism of barefoot people—everyone is promiscuous
    upstairs.
Oh feet, poise in repose, mit luftpost, glands and serifs for the
    legs.

Jungian days—a pair of shoes *sur le tapis*
manfully complete the narrative with no legs attached!
What could they be doing what could they be doing
Will they shave themselves on this personal day?

But we live in an age where these shoes are yours.
Flying in the face of whatever (mutable) sumptuary laws are
    going down,
please (gratitude relieving stress) accept them the both of them
for free in rosy tissue paper I beseech in size 7-1/2 medium left
    and right, one for each foot.

Dean and Later Bishop

Listen to how we indulged in a hare-brained scheme of trying to
establish a college on the other side of the Atlantic
in the Bermudas to proselytize and educate
the Indians who lived on the mainland. We tried to transport
ourselves to Bermuda for that. We believed that Parliament
would actually make good the money they had promised
to found this college. One whom we took with us
was Mr. Smibert, a distinguished Scottish painter,
so that he could teach the Indians the history of architecture.
Accordingly we with our effects set sail for Rhode Island,
a strategic situation for approaching Bermuda,
and were a long time blundering about on the ocean,
until Captain Cobb the incompetent landed us in Virginia
instead, where we observed with satisfaction
the College of William and Mary and where William Byrd

opined that we were very romantic. Eventually in Rhode Island
we studied the Narragansett Indians, as a way of preparing
for the experience of Bermuda, and we visited
Dighton Rock. It is covered with ancient letters.

Our old dear Dean Swift his Miss Van Homrigh
had left us four thousand pounds by way of a gracious
and providential bequest, and so we had begun our enterprise.
But it became clearer and clearer in letters from England
that the allocation from Parliament was not forthcoming, nor
    would it ever be,
because it was going to be used as the dowry of Princess
    Something.
Mr. Smibert went to Boston to paint his pictures
and married Miss Williams who was a great-granddaughter

of Anne Bradstreet, the Tenth Muse Lately Sprung Up in
   America.
He did not marry Miss Handcock, the friend of our wife.
He designed Faneuil Hall. And he bade us goodbye at Boston
as we returned home to become Bishop of Cloyne in Ireland
and never saw him again whom we had met
so many years ago in Italy, after we had already articulated the
   sum of our philosophy,
when we journeyed through Apulia in our relative youth with
   St. George Ashe,
and ate pesto every day and looked around libraries for Greek
   manuscripts and carefully observed the afflicted doing the
   tarantella.

Off Gems Bund

if u cn rd ths u cn gt a gd jb
& leaping into the sack at Muldoon's Point
for Eine Kleine Nachtmusik, so I ask shreenk
what *he* seenk. He say Caramba! No affect! (I weel keel heem.)
Seenk of zees now only bot choss zees once.

This me repugnates, by San Pedro (Castenets in Galilee)!
bot ozzer eediots why zey no write? *sigilium*
universitatis Pennsylvaniensis, dixit. I repine.
"Someday my brother's works will be translated into German."
(José, can you see?) *Bonnuit, tailleur!* Home, Gems! we senk
    [Get*] vor promises!

Exploring Unknown Territory

Exploring unknown territory wearing Admiral Peary's earflaps
is a moot beginning to a metaphysical poem.
There doesn't seem to be an explanation of how the poet came
into possession of the earflaps
or any particular virtue to them that could rub off on the poet
and make her or him soar in realms of blue.

Admiral Peary would probably not have countenanced the blue
movie or *Fear-of-Flying*-type books,
not that he was attracted to "realms of gold" either.
But it is quite in order to lie, to steadfastly present an
explanation of the earflaps,
as if it were just what had happened, making the reader totally
comfortable.

*   *   *

One of the important points in Boethius from a stylistic, not
philosophic, point of view, is that in the great length of *The
Consolation of Philosophy*, and in the subtle structure, with its
poignant emotional steps, he alternates passages of verse and
prose. The variety and multiplicity of the universe is its joy as
well as its puzzlement. Boethius knew this well. This is a leaf
out of his book.

*   *   *

My husband, who is probably my best critic,
is not absolutely sure whether Peary discovered the South or
North but believes it was the North Pole.

*   *   *

ADMIRAL PEARY: Millicent has fine hands and firm,
                  creamlike skin.

23

MY HUSBAND:	Is Millicent a relative?
ADMIRAL PEARY:	Well, yes and no.
MILLICENT:	Here are the earflaps. The band fits snugly over the headpiece, and then the strap goes under the chin, so.
MY HUSBAND:	I hope you have a splendid trip. I must say I rather wish I were going with you. Goodbye, sir.
ADMIRAL PEARY:	Goodbye.

* * *

Documentation of sources: a weary time, a weary time. Some kind of freshening, of loosening of the sensibilities is necessary, sort of what Boethius did, in order to constantly make the connection between the source (*fons*) of the information, and the conclusions gathered (*electa*) from the information. How is the material presented? The process of documentation can be very exacting.

* * *

Dear Sir:

Please send me a pair of earflaps identical with the ones you sent me in March of 1907. I have found these handsome and serviceable.

Yours very truly,
Admiral Peary

* * *

MY HUSBAND:	Have you looked up Admiral Peary?
I:	No, I was busy. Does Millicent bother you at all?
MY HUSBAND:	No, I think she's lovely. But I really believe that it is one-sided to write about Boethius and not write about Isidore of Seville.

* * *

I don't know what you think you will find. I think it is
dangerous and stupid to go away like that. I think you should
be careful about charts. The scar on your foot will be
recognized as you enter cities. You will have dreams again
whenever you go away. It is a great risk.

* * *

MY HUSBAND: Mr. Ashbery, would you look at my
                poem?
JOHN ASHBERY: Sure. (Reads aloud.)

One of the Nice Things About Winter
BY MASON KNOX
The garbage cans don't smell
And nothing grows in them no more.

Now you read one of mine.

MY HUSBAND: Thank you. (Reads silently.) This is full of
                French!
JOHN ASHBERY: They aren't the same poem.
MY HUSBAND: Why do you say you write romantic
                poems and not metaphysical poems? It
                seems to me that if you write poems that
                are commenting on themselves as they are
                being written and read, that's about as
                metaphysical as you can get.
JOHN ASHBERY: Ah! you are saying that the earflaps
                prevent hearing!
MY HUSBAND: The earflaps?

* * *

A picaresque adventure. My husband and I are twenty and
nineteen, respectively. It is some time ago. We are walking down
Main Street in Stonington, Connecticut, from his parents' house

to his grandmother's house. We have blocks of wood and sandpaper in our hands which we are sanding down so that we can paint Russian Orthodox icons on them. A lady is sitting in an upstairs window of one of the houses. She says to someone in the room, "There goes that stupid Mason Knox and his stupid girlfriend doing something stupid."

* * *

ADMIRAL PEARY: Welcome aboard, sir.

JOHN ASHBERY: Thank you, but I will not come aboard. I am quite happy here.

ADMIRAL PEARY: But you'll freeze.

JOHN ASHBERY: I won't freeze. Before you left, did you see Mason Knox?

ADMIRAL PEARY: Well, yes. He was in New York. He was reading a paper.

JOHN ASHBERY: How was he?

ADMIRAL PEARY: Fine.

* * *

ADMIRAL PEARY: What is this?

G. M. HOPKINS: This is the random grim forge. I wrote about it in "Felix Randal."

ADMIRAL PEARY: I don't see why it's random.

G. M. HOPKINS: John Ashbery does not write metaphysical poems.

ADMIRAL PEARY: Oh. What is the forge doing here.

G. M. HOPKINS: Ashbery would say it was part of the documentation. I am willing to give him that.

* * *

MY HUSBAND: Now that you've blown our cover, I suppose you will put Admiral Peary's earflaps on the Russian Orthodox icon.

26

I:	No. Here comes Mr. Ashbery.
JOHN ASHBERY:	(Very quietly, to my husband; we are at a large, elaborate party.) I have done some poems involving Isidore of Seville's *Etymologies*. In this work he gives a great many false etymologies of words and concepts, but the etymologies are only a pretext for presenting volumes of information that he wanted to get across anyway.
MY HUSBAND:	You don't need to tell me about old Isidore. I'm a canonist.
JOHN ASHBERY:	No kidding. Then would you please explain this parchment to me.
MY HUSBAND:	Sure, I'll try.

*   *   *

I have a college classmate who is an expert in the care of decaying documents. During the Venetian flood she worked for CRIA and saved many treasures by wonderful methods. She wrote and said we should roll out the parchment as though it were piecrust. Then we should tack it lightly all around the edges, and iron it at a low setting. She says we have to be very careful with the ink.

*   *   *

MY HUSBAND:	Which parchment?
I:	Well, it isn't parchment. The part about John Ashbery and Isidore was a dream, that's all.
MY HUSBAND:	For God's sake, what is it, then?
I:	Xerox paper. I got it out of the wastebasket. It has a little writing on the other side. —It's very difficult about the ending.

27

MY HUSBAND:	I don't see why.
I:	Well, in any normal thing you write, you say what you've discovered, and why you wanted to get into it in the first place. You finish with a mush sentence: thus we see that Walker and Jones (1966) could not fail to conclude, etc.
MY HUSBAND:	I wish you would end with Millicent.
I:	That's not a bad idea.

*   *   *

MILLICENT:	First, I take the cream cheese, softened, and beat in the sifted flour and baking powder. —There's someone at the door.
ADMIRAL PEARY:	Millicent? Millicent, my dear.
MILLICENT:	You're back! Extraordinary. Everyone will be delighted.
ADMIRAL PEARY:	Get your things.
MILLICENT:	What? Right now?
ADMIRAL PEARY:	Right now. We're going over to the Smithsonian.

28

Log of the Snow Star

Chief asked if I'd go aloft, and in spite of boots
and other impedimenta I said yes
and went. The lower shrouds are easy and over
the top you go and then begins a single
line of ratlines. Tilberry right behind me,
so I said You go on ahead, and this he did.

Then Tilberry handed me the gasket
and Pedersen said to put it through, in fact.
Look LOOK said Tilberry there's corposants.

What's got into this old grump. From his nails,
from the spars, the dull light, the legend in hand:
St. Elmo's Fire. We didn't say it was.
Where did Tilberry get it. We didn't
say anything into the sky, bright before snow.

Then climbed down slowly but not so slowly
as to hold up Tilberry, who was climbing down
above me. Chief came out and called us
as for coffee. Made chafing gear on watch.
Learned Swedish profanity from Chips, who tried
to kiss me. Christine and I that night
also out on the jibboom; but up on the fore
t'gallant yard the schooner the *Snow Star*
is her own sailing model in the wand of minor planets.

Customs

We are going to la shirty Scala and il spiffy Duomo,
together in Italy for the very first time.
Dog-eared Rome of the Caesars, warm to the touch,
where we dine, *etc.*, with a connection of Victor Emmanuel!
(italics mine), and I write it all down in the back of my little

Comp Lit notebook. How about we go over to the Vatican
and look at the penguins? How about we make some phone
    calls?
to Arthur Fonzarelli? How about some diet Kahlua?
How about I keep my mouth shut? too late, too late.

The children pretend to be dogs, and the dogs pretend to be
    laundry.
When you see dear old So-and-So, please give him my regards.
"My sense of it was somewhat grotesque." "The woman is a
    vicissitude."
Hic Vicarius Filii Dei suum flip-flop *perdidit.*

Now their sweethearts have become business associates and
    their wifies actuaries;
latterly we are still stranded in our Expedition-Weight
    Polypropylene Balaclavas
at the lovely Signorina's or here in Town X maybe,
in the crepuscular rain, bosky fells, gelato di pesto, with no
    money to get home.

The Urn

The cold urn signifies that Nonnie never
back across the NaCl H_2O
shall venture nor the fardeled spaniel persever
with his lemon liquid eye bones to bestow:
the old consul has deserved well of the state
and is translated into winter quarters
in Cisalpine Gaul who what with her deckled borders
and all is some eclectic numinous broad
(polemics billow forth and plays are written
—the urn's the province of the orthopod)
comfortable and fecund and ornate
yet chafed in the gizzard by Armorican Britain.
    Chalk one up for the caterpillars of
      the commonwealth and their parataxis, love.

Gerhard Thorpe, Male Nurse

A source of ill-concealed speculation at St. Pancras Hospital was the regard in which Gerhard Thorpe held Dr. Ruskin, its freshman anesthesiologist. To Gerhard, Dr. Ruskin's strong glossy brown hair and sensitive eyes seemed alive and made his blood course through his veins and return to his heart. The hospital proper had been designed at the turn of the century by Meservey, a pupil of Wright. One seldom associates dogs with hospitals, and yet St. Pancras had a corps of ten, which were actually the darling pets of staff. The Lab had its own Lab Labs. Gerhard's Newfoundland, Ch. Fjord's Restive Thought, was accomplished in the Heimlich Maneuver. Dr. Ruskin had a pair of English setters. A lot of ritzy snob talk took place over the dogs and a lot of nosy snooping about Gerhard and Dr. Ruskin, especially from Nanny and Nanny Gruffum.

The nurse held riboflavin samples and looked adoringly at Dr. R. He had grown up in the medical business and he liked it, for various good reasons. He patted the mighty head of a Lab Lab. Leslie Ruskin turned to him her fine smile and asked, "Will we meet at International AMA in England?"

"England," he replied, "Yes, and I'm not looking forward to their cold toast in little bike racks, little slices of masonite to ruin decent hot eggs with."

Gerhard and Leslie conducted trysts in the laundry room, which was huge and cosy and full of Meservey's secret nookeries. The lock was perpetually broken, so they put *Books in Print* against the door. Some weekends they spent at Tenley's. At Blenheim an AMA party undulated and surged with booze and pre-lust. Gerhard munched on a hot dog with relish. Sexism reared its fanged head in the person of Rupert Moncrieff, M.D. Bishop Gumbleton was there.

"I've got Gantricin, which brings in two hundred thou per

annum and a Quando and six Ruptos," said Moncrieff. "Isn't that great? What's your name?"

Dr. Ruskin was ready with a retort. "It's *not* great. The people with the political power and the money are MORALLY OBLIGED to take care of the poor people and old and handicapped and so forth!"—toying with her netsuke.

"You're the best looking female subversive in the whole AMA!" said Dr. M., who liked E. Power Biggs. "Come and drown my sorrows."

But a wall of pathologists suddenly veiled them from one another, and Gerhard, too, who went to the pool to swim laps. Of course no dogs were allowed on this trip. Moncrieff appeared at the top of Gerhard's ladder wearing a meat suit and flippers. "Maybe I'll punch Moncrieff in the nose," thought Gerhard on the plane back. "Then again, maybe I won't." At home they found the hospital inventory was nearly complete. Shiny and sedate on the shelves sat drums of horse liniment, carabiners, the *Analecta Turabiana,* all things needful.

A Pink Man wheeled Mrs. Asimov into surgery. "I am no relation to Isaac," she said, "but I would I were," she said to her roommate Mrs. Farley. "Have you read his essay on the platypus?" Mrs. Farley was in a coma. There were so many vehicles in life. Gerhard for one possessed a disgraceful 1969 mauve Volvo sedan.

A hamlike blocking figure crashed violently around the hospital corner, skirting Mrs. Asimov but against poor Leslie in the half-light, knocking from her ringed and so dazzling hand a Petri dish of ossified gizzards. This was Rupert. Leslie screamed. He is the Hippocratic Oaf, she thought but forebore to say. Orderlies removed him, fortunately, and the government presently annexed some although not all of his condominiums by eminent domain.

And now Leslie and Gerhard waited in their doctor's waiting room for annual checkups, best prevention. A buzzer buzzed. "Seuss Demento and Scholl," said the receptionist aristo-

cratically into the receiver. "A polyp? Would you like to say
a little more about that?" The doctor was very late but they
got clean bills of health and no bill, inasmuch as they were
vocationally speaking in health care services as a profession.
"Blenheim has the biggest living rooms in the world," said
Leslie. She was reading a biography of Stanley Baldwin. Well
pleased, they made their way to the St. Pancras laundry. Let us
leave them there. Nanny and Nanny Gruffum cleaned up the
ossified gizzards, endeavoring to give satisfaction. Then as so
often they did Sortes Telephoniae, in which they never, never got
caught.

Lizzie Borden Through Art and Literature

Somewhat to the east of East Providence, driving along 195,
the USS *Massachusetts* rides at (permanent) anchor
in the brackish river-harbor of Fall River
(her sister the *Constitution* further to the north
in the Bay Colony slapping similarly).
Myth once there (in 1892, Clio in abeyance), cruel and untrue
    as it turned out,
sprang full blown from the old brow of the coast-to-coast
newspaper-swallowing populace!

Bright leavings of hammers Elizabeth Borden grasped,
much as was Carthage blitzed, or Egypt asped,
to whose male parent-unit to administer
buffets twoscore revealed in quatrain sinister.
Which when the principal looked upon amain,
the surrogate womb full forty shee againe.

The original manuscript is as it were a palimpsest,
since the "piece" is the instant art of oral-formulaic illiterate
    tradition
featuring: 1) formulas, 2) incremental repetition, 3) the single
    epic hero in conflict with the dark adversary, 4) abrupt
    juxtaposition instead of subtle transition;
but it hardly stopped there. Ballets danced for her (acquitted-in-
    a-court-of-law) guilt,
clouded subsequent reminiscences of impeccable statespersons,
celluloid spent, dazzling and mock-heroic tours-de-force of New
    Faces and the Kingston Trio,
good reads, and sensible histories of the Industrial Revolution.

35

The Farley Family

Heed the Words

"Chaffee gets out of the monastery tomorrow," said Mrs. Farley, "and it's just thrilling."

"You gave him a yurt," said Augusta. She and Chaffee had been being nice to each other for years.

"I am very mad, Augusta, that you don't ask me all about it. Hand over the sherry. Here is kitty. Kitty went typies this morning on IBM. THREE FAITHFUL YOUTHS WE NOW WILL LEND YOU UPON YOUR JOURNEY THEY'LL ATTEND YOU. I had a go at it, Augusta, but it's no go. THOUGH YOUNG IN YEARS THESE YOUTHS SO FAIR. . . ."

"HEED THE WORDS OF WISDOM RARE!" bellowed Augusta. It was an idiotic chorus out of *The Magic Flute*. Mrs. Farley asked Chaffee if he would help entertain Mrs. Fenton, a new neighbor. But Mrs. Fenton said, "Go away; I don't want to be entertained." She consented, however, to let him drive her home from a picnic they had. "I'm going to call you Chaffee from now on," said Mrs. Fenton, "and I want you to call me Helen— I mean Ruth."

* * *

Dear Janet,

Excuse me sincerely, I am very confused not to have written more rapidly, but I prepared my exam "BEP Sanitaire et Social." You know, this exam is important for my comrades but not for me. I set my candidature for going to a school of "Beaux-Arts" in Bourges. In September I'll have an exam where I must show to the jury some paint, sketch made at the charcoal, etc. In France, it's very hot. I have finished to go to school in May, so I am in vocation still in October.

What do you do this summer? I am very happy, because my mother is going to get married. My futur stepfather is very nice. He have, as my mother, children who are nineteen, twenty-two. My mother will stop to travel. Perhaps my sister will get married and so my mother that which would be marvelous. Two Marriages. Do you understand French? You can, perhaps, write to me in French, just some sentences if you have some difficulties. I adore to speak and write English but I make many of faults. Perhaps a day I'll go to your big country but now I must leave you.

Ariane.

*   *   *

Granny Farley

Granny Farley loves her chubsters—she gives them peppermints when Mother doesn't know. First a slice of carrot. Then a peppermint. Just like the baby woodchucks who open their little mouths, and the baby robins open theirs, and then in goes the carrot, and in goes the oops! try again. Granny never saw such good carrot-chompers. The baby woodchucks wish they had such THERE we go for Granny's story.

There was once a princess who lived in Paris, and her favorite animal was baby bobcats. But there were none in France, so the princess asked her father the king to send to Connecticut for lots of bobcats, because that's where the best ones came from and still do. And when they got there they had little reddish puffs of fur all over them, so the princess named them the Redgolden Beautifications. Then one day when she was playing with the bobcats in the palace garden, a fiery dragon came and tried to eat everybody up. The king was on a journey to Palestine and the royal servants were asleep. So the princess threw her wastebasket and her typewriter and her watering can into the dragon's horrible mouth and he choked to death at once. All the baby bobcats rejoiced with lots of good things to eat. And under the covers we go tucked right in tight, with fuzzy friendly animals and pillows and sweet repose and kisses and air kisses from the door.

* * *

The Federal Period

"But it isn't an Early American eagle," insisted Peggy. "The Early American Period is 1619 FOB Holland, up to and including the Revolution. There it stops. They didn't put up eagles until—oh—the 1840s."

"Well, whaddaya know," said Chaffee. They were at Town Meeting. This year everybody had name tags. Worley (Worley Farley, brother to Chaffee) moved that the minutes of the last Town Meeting be not read; Peggy seconded this. It was so voted. Chaffee snuggled close to Peggy and breathed in her brown hair. What a meeting, how boring, how terrific to look around and see everybody.

"Anyway Jamestown (1607) is much earlier than Plymouth and Virginia Dare too. Or you could get into Vikings and Irishmen and Indians."

They were making *much* too much noise for Town Meeting and of course were asked to leave. Chaffee's car took them away through the delicious countryside of the Federal Period, past lots of eagles real and otherwise.

"Mrs. Fenton lives over there. I drove her home once. oops," he said. "Your brow is furrowed and green."

"Not at all."

"I am not carrying on with her. Mother asked me to be nice." All knew that Mrs. Fenton was haggish.

"You're the nicest Farley."

Peggy and Chaffee pulled into the (terrible) driveway. Mrs. Farley was away for the week at a medievalists' clambake; she was reading a paper on the Venerable Bede in Muncie, Indiana, of all things, and then Bird Camp. So Peggy and Chaffee had pretty much the run of the place.

* * *

A Landmark Case

"Listen, there were these seven families with seven teenage daughters in the city of Eugene, Oregon. The girls got together and forced their parents to throw them a huge coming-out party, since they were coming of age.

"The party was at a splendid downtown hotel. There was lots of lobster salad and Olympic Peninsula salmon and oysters, and oceans of champagne. Some guests got pretty drunk and horsed around a lot and some took some drugs. They broke chandeliers and tables and the columns around the dance floor.

"Then the drunk guests got still drunker and wilder and went out into the street. They threw rocks at streetlights and crashed their cars through the fronts of municipal buildings, destroying a lot of public property. The police could do nothing to stop them.

"So the city brought suit against the seven girls to recover damages. Do you want to know what the case was called?"

"Oh yes, Chaffee."

"Eugene V. Debs."

* * *

The Dead Cat Act

When Samuel Farley at the age of sixteen chose to sell his electric trains for good green lettuce, he telephoned a hobby and collector store in a nearby city to get an appraisal.

Janet Farley sat at the dining-room table doing Latin lessons. She wrote *flammis acribus addictis*—"having been subjected to sour flames." Then she wrote *flammis farlibus addictis*. Sam and Dad got her to move so they could spread out the electric trains.

39

Warlock Farley, the largest cat in the county, entered the room and lay down under this table of which I speak.

Janet was wearing a cream and gray outfit, gray pants with a soft tweed blazer and a lovely pleated cream-colored shirt, and gold ear hoops. Warlock was the gray of these pants, very fluffy beyond his actual great size. He liked to lie under the table and do a dead cat act, and this he did now.

The hobby man arrived at the door, bringing his wife. The former was a pleasure to have around, said Dad later, and the latter a mean Home Ec person. The wife looked at Warlock. His bottom half was stomach up and his feet were up in the air, revealing to the sight all his reproductive organs. His top half was totally swiveled 180 degrees with a look (fake) of ugly pain on the part of his fat face that was visible between his front paws. The wife stared at Warlock all the time the financial transaction was taking place.

Janet Farley rose from her armchair. "The Board of Health will probably be here soon," she said. The wife, dear reader, didn't say anything.

*   *   *

The True Rag

Janet came into my room and said that all the seams were out of her blue jeans. Then they are the True Rag, I said; but I was wrong.

The True Rag had been found at Glastonbury. It had been found at Bury St. Edmunds. It had been found by goats on Skiathos, Greece, as people sat in the twilit café, sipping *bouzouki* and listening to the *metaxa*. It had been found at Aix-les-Bains and Juan-les-Pins. But Mrs. Farley proved conclusively that it had been found at her summer house in New Mexico, because *she found it,* and sold it to the Yale textile collection for a huge undisclosed sum, and she said that she used the proceeds of the sale to help some medical students from the University of Chicago with a special pilot project.

Shrines have been erected at the sites where the True Rag was found. Pilgrims to the English and French shrines remove their shoes on entering and they always hear a choir singing when they view the True Rag. Those who have seen it say it is made of a kind of gossamer, that it does not glow in the dark, and that it has French seams (which is a point for the French claim).

The pilgrims to Skiathos say that the True Rag is made of rough shepherd's cloth, and is terribly worn but not at all dirty. Mrs. Farley told the *New York Times* that the True Rag is made of plain gray silk, not shiny, and that there is a border of small white flowers along the selvage. The True Rag is not on exhibit at Yale.

There is a beautiful legend about the True Rag. When St. Francis was an old man, he had a vision of Jesus's boyhood. Jesus was helping St. Joseph clean up the carpentry shop. When some other children came by and made fun of His gentleness and meekness, St. Joseph threw a firkin of boiled linseed oil on them and told them to go away. But Jesus quietly rebuked His Guardian and, taking the True Rag from where it hung on the wall, carefully cleaned the boiled linseed oil off the dripping children, so that they were as clean as they had been before.

* * *

At "The Elms"

Years later Ariane and Nick live in a tiny chimney-pot apartment in Boston which everyone calls "The Elms." They are entertaining to dinner Janet and a cowboy! of hers and others. Nick puts his face into the steam of satiny sweet-and-sour pork and Ariane grossly says, "I didn't know people had hair on *top* of their noses," and Nick hipchecks her (Boston is a skating town). Nick has sung with the Grease Monkeys until recently, when onerous work—he is a medical underwriter, whatever that is, for New England Life—obliged him to give up the evenings with the GMs, who feel the loss.

The cowboy is extremely handsome and also nice to people.

He asks Nick about the architecture of "The Elms" and they
talk about decaying red sandstone houses in Roxbury. Janet is
wearing a bedspread pinned with an opal. Everyone likes the
cowboy, secretly relieved that he doesn't tell them about the
range. Ariane puts a spinach soufflé surrounded by tiny carrots
on the table. Nick tells Janet she is Florence of Arabia. The
cowboy lights the candles with lots of help from Janet. God
send all girlfriends such boyfriends and also vice versa.

* * *

Noodle Island

I went out in the shallop to paint the horizon from Noodle
Island, the city, actually. My paints smooshed together in the
chop, I wot not how. Nathl with me, grumpy but he excels all
the students. I "went blind after 1746 of failing eyesight."
Hirschl & Adler in NYC offered this last [he means the
landscape, I guess] for 950 thousand, much later—1982; even
Jane, distinguished resource person, essay on the *solidus* (????!)
gasped at the sum. Of course only the portraits are decent. I
think sometimes the Dean is full of rant and cant (Kant?? ha
ha). Nat is amounting to something despite his angry tongue. I
wish I were at Fabia's but it will never happen again, etc.
Probably she's in the Moravian Cistern now. I do my Brigadoon
pose for all the Americans, wee mites o' Scots bairns i' th' tarn.
Many many more portraits. Copley is too rosy for words and
the taste of the country is going to hell in a handbasket.

* * *

In Brussels

Reverend Monsignor spends now the evening of his life at the
Prokura in Brussels, where the twilit days are enriched by the
visits of students and old friends who always return to him
from their foundation stations in Indonesia and elsewhere. To

them he gives counsel and humorous good advice and then he
sees them on their way into the provinces which he has helped
to shape. A dream (again) of supposes, remembers, read oaters,
go sleep. Forasmuch as about him lie grammars untouched, all
the reports which he will not complete, these are his trinkets
and cenotaphs to something he imagines every day.

How often they ask him to tell them stories of Chaffee and the
like; but he does not consent to do so. The schools are closed
for the farming season and many disputes. Child labor laws do
not inhibit little feet from padding to and from the market. It is
lush and full midsummer and yet who can account for his
tiredness, which seems to spread like arms upon the banisters of
public buildings and shadows.

Sestina for Bishop Seabury

The engraving of Bishop Seabury on the Seabury Deanery
letterhead stationery (the southeastern Seabury
Deanery being a division of the Diocese of Connecticut
[Episcopal]) is too early to be taken from a painting by Daniel
Huntington and shows the subject as stationary
—but not in his father's foundation at Poquetanuck—

and hermeneutic not hieratic. At Poquetanuck
—well, Santiago de Poquetanuck, in this Deanery
(founded in 1720)—where history seems stationary,
you will not find the sepulcher of Seabury,
but at Santiago de New London. Arnaut Daniel
invented the sestina but has nothing to do with Connecticut,

inasmuch as he was a Provençal troubadour. The Connecticut
Wits were not connected with Poquetanuck.
The contemporaneous *Robinson Crusoe*, Daniel
Defoe's best-seller, may well have circulated in the Deanery;
but it's unlikely to have appealed to Bishop Seabury
and is too revolutionary to appear on the Deanery stationery.

Whose Tory polity remaining not exactly stationary,
according to Sanford's *History of Connecticut*
(p. 239), there interposed for Seabury

44

"serious difficulties" far from Poquetanuck,
who maintained his spirituality and that of what became the
    Deanery
by reciting (perhaps) another Samuel—Samuel Daniel,

or preaching on Samuel I and II and on Daniel,
as even in the engraving of which we speak on the stationery,
for the regulation ninety-four minutes. The Seabury Deanery
today consists of sixteen parishes of Connecticut,
the smallest of which is Santiago de Poquetanuck.
Thou shalt rest, and stand in thy lot, says Bishop Seabury.

The right hand of the surgeon and Eli, Bishop Seabury,
rests on the book. He isn't your basic Daniel
Boone or Daniel Webster figure from Poquetanuck,
but a faithful plenary likeness on ordinary stationery,
agent of the continental succession and Connecticut
dispensation, as who should remark in this Deanery:

Who will the sound toss, the sea bury, children of the Deanery,
natives of Connecticut, auditors of that text from Daniel,
stationary Pequots and Wampanoags along the trail through
    Poquetanuck?

Golfe de
S. Laurens

Anticosti ou
l'Assompti
on

Golfe

C. des
guille

Gr.
Baye

C du Grat

B. d'Orge

B. de S.
Georges

B. Blanche

de la Conception.

Terrë

C. Francois

Neuve

Gr. Golfe
de la Sphere

C. Breton

C. de Roye
I. de S. Pol
C. de S. Laurens

B. de S. Claire

B. de S. Marie

des Trepasses

C. de Re

Breton

. de
arseau

I. de Sable

To Newfoundland

Rural poverty makes for maritime enterprise, they say. This is why over and over ships from Scandinavian ports left for the New World, manned by many men and dogs. You can imagine that the circumstances of (a) being tempest-tossed and blown off course while trying to get to Greenland, and (b) missing Greenland altogether, and (c) discovering Newfoundland, were an occasion for quantities of poetry writing by those involved. Some of the poetry was terrible and highly inaccurate. Few have the gift. Here are examples:

DOGS:
    Bough! wough! whose dogs are we
    whan al our maysters are frae hame
    or off to Greenland on the sea

    We hae nae laird We have no lord
    We all are equal in this place
    Bough! wough! the glancing chop
    betides wi' froth the lop-eared face

    In curragh rough or beamy knarr
    the crew are all impressed
    and row beside the Newfoundland dogs
    to Newfoundland in the west

    Let cairns rain down upon ye
    bearing petroglyphs
    Let ogham be in your ears
    Let there be mastiffs

VIKING CAPTAIN:
    Maybe we will emulate (and not tell the priest)

Radwald the Wuffing our distinguished
   cousin
He received Christ but held on tight
to all the old gods just in case

I have to speak in quatrains
because I am a protagonist
The things we did were horrifying
but we were brave and they're over with

Farewell to unfair Harald Fairhair
He thinks to unite all the kinglets is
   grand
He must do it without my historical help
I'm going to Newfoundland

CREW: Tae Aberdour, frae Norrowa
Tae ony place but here
We'll tak the hand-carved artifact
the replica of the spear

We'll tak the powdered reindeer horn
the elvish herbish brume
with kindergarten spindlewhorl
we seek our new-found hame

To Newfoundland, to Newfoundland
with Viking dogs and sleds
with Nordic thought from Tacitus
and helmets on our heads

   I chewed up the captain's bone skates because he didn't let me
go on the inland voyage. I am a strong Newf now and can do
everything that Bladethorpe can do and as fast, and I don't get

my leggings tangled up like he does. Lots of Newves get to go at age two but not me. The Indian dogs are odd and not particularly friendly. Their hair is pretty short, perhaps because of poor diet. Some of us mated with them anyway—that's how it goes. The settlement is going to be huge and will fill up the valley of L'Anse-aux-Meadowes. It is like a dog dish full of the sea. I chased some deer off—they can run eleven miles in fifty minutes. The fishing is the absolute greatest, miles of water up to the knees teeming with salmon and adolescent codfish. I'd just as lief stay forever.

Here's how we operate. The fish swim right up to shore to eat fallen tree blossoms. We hide in packs behind the trees. Suddenly we all charge in and grab them. Every little dog gets his fish. MANY DOGS HERE, we wrote in the sand in our *futhark, so* happy and crammed full of dinner. The master said, "Footing of divers great beasts!"

Bladethorpe is too arrogant; he's the Dream of the Rude. He says that the celebrated dog that met St. Brendan in the New World was one of the Bladethorpe of Bladethorpe Newfies. Anyone who believes that Brendan stuff is crazy. Bladethorpe has a little blanket made of *wadmal*. It is so effete but he's into it; the starboard watch confided all this to me. He Bladethorpe also thinks the Beothuk Indians are related to Beowulf. What an idiot.

There was a Great Auk Roast in a grove of hackmatack with games beforehand, poetry afterward. It was part of The Thing. Several Beothuk came and in an "amicable gesture" poured seawater over the master's head. You can bet Bladethorpe saw this as some kind of rite. The Beothuk heaved cornbread at us. To make this, maize is brayed in a mortar, mixed with water into dough, and separated into cakes which are cooked on a hot stone covered with pebbles. The poet was brushing a quadrant of my "peltry." He had scalded himself on the chowder and so was temporarily mute. There is nothing in this world as good as the dog-backrubs given by Thornhild. She is a beautiful woman who stirs puddings in the smelly kitchen. I love to be there—she fluffs my ruff. "If grownup Newfies look like puppies, and they do, what do Newf puppies look like, I ask," she asked.

I like to participate in Thornhild's life to a degree. She told this provenance of herself. She had had a sweetheart back home who was conscribed to Harald's army. She told him she'd tie back her hair and put on men's clothing and pass as his comrade as they marched along. No one would ever know. Wouldn't he let her go with him (it grieved her heart so, and she said it three times). He said no my love no (*na min leof na*) three times and then gave her his final answer: no my love no. This is how Thornhild came to the New World—to lose lost love. She also learned to cook whelk.

One of the feast day games went like this. Olaf, a sailor, nailed his boots to two barrel-staves. Then he got out in the wake of the (supple, clinker-built) pinnace tied to a line by his middle. He stood up on the barrel-staves and got towed around for hours, flukes spooming fore and aft among the bergs and growlers. Many barks along the coast that day. We observed the swells. Another game was to make oubliettes for caribou.

The bergs are like burgs. They used to be part of the northern glaciers; then the glaciers calved and the bergs came here. The sailors call them "flyaway islands." Birds live on them: ptarmigan, guillemot, merganser, auk, and puffin. I was disgusted to see the trout eat mice! I've eaten a lot of trout! Give me substantial caribou bones any day. I like to chew them up immediately so I can have some nostalgia about them.

There is one more strange thing to tell. The master and our party were sailing along the coast right near and something gleamed. It was a uniped. It came jumping down to the boat and shot an arrow into the very center of the master's heart. He prophesied and later he died. The poet was along and wrote:

The men were chasing
and it is true
a uniped
down to the beach
This weird creature
streaked away
sank in water
Hear, o ship master!

Thornhild and I did not know what to think of that.
Bladethorpe met us when the boat came ashore and told us the
names of his children: Grommet, Rage, Bloodthorpe,
Toastcruncher, Petit Nord, Main Tempest, Mound, Biffures,
Boney's Rescue, The Fractious One. Indian Branch: Eskimo
Whooper, Boffin of Baffin. The red line of the Newfies descends
from the Eskimo dogs. Anyway, there you have it—quadruped,
biped, and uniped, all pretty much bilaterally symmetrical.
Thornhild and I developed Olaf's "theme," splashing around on
the beach. She was throwing an oar in for me to fetch. With the
oar on this feast day we wrote in the sand what was doubtless
in every heart:

THE MORE TERRE
THE LESS NEUVE

Teeth

Teeth being situated as they in fact are so close to the brain
and thus permanently indentured to it exercise atavistic violence
on a cube steak say or Lillian Russell or newfangled
   comestibles.
This memoralizes of teeth reason and passion. If *you* were they,

what would you like to chew best? This tooth is named
   Barbara,
dreamy and respectable among colleagues, sandwiched
   anymore
between gums and gum. The wantons selves disport
cheerily in series and in parallel, hard by their "friend," the ear.

They pronounce Chidiock Tichbourne for us in committee
and gleam, the foul white radishes of time.
Sometimes help to say, "Set in 10 on 12 point Palatino."
Teeth finally are the stars (on a loom) of memory and the cusp
   of youth.

The Heart

Send the First-Amendment Heart (to the showers glistening)
on the Fifth-Amendment sleeve as it were a corporate ensign

logo PDQ back to me. For the figural
witness which I floated is not more cost-effective

than principle and we ought to remain
Brown V. Board of Ed about problem-solving

in any (hapless) event. I'll as a floral summat receive it *a capella*
home, hardly artillery as some. Now so far

heart, flag, and rose, *res publica,* the bower,
the expected to take seriously. The thorny

pillow is furled in the bosom of the legislature
(what a dicy GRE and the mirror of a Hasselblad

at this writing. Apocalyptic condescends to allegory, believe us,
so wartish bombastic don whose throwaways are
    foregrounded).

Tassels and all affixed, load ammo rebate FOB
with Hu-Kwa up in Audi, *avoir du poids* of oxgang;

but I'll take the Fifth, bolting from League to League:
"The silken veil of crystal is the closest

thing to nothing between your lips and the wine."
That's what they tell me anyhow in Peoria
and Pawtucket regardless, in a *Doppelgänger* of capillary
    action.

Movement Along the Frieze

Who are these people who have got their grammar and their
  diction levels
the way they want them. Who are their sweethearts
and who is their friend that they call up in McKeesport
and say something to. A plain tale. Please like their work.
Please like what men and women and children present the
line-breaks of. How did they get their act together
in the matter of sentence fragments, which are sacraments,
and of all those Nortony things, in their English-teacher
  costumes
or barn clothes and out partying in Bayónne, New Jersey,
  writing stuff down all the time.
Please anyway read what they brought out of the despair
of the boringness of expected word order and what got printed
  with margins
on four sides of it, in what somebody else, a graphics person,
figured out for a typeface; oh please like all these
and the cover of paper which is supposed to decompose
so that they will have something to write their elegiac and
  mutability
poems about, some of them even MID-party arguing in oral
  comma splice
that written comma splice is a form of parallel structure
and so not only justified but welcome! and others loudly
  disagreeing
totally. (And one of the noisiest avers that incremental repetition
is a form of parallel structure!) Some write syntax down goofy
and then go back and put profundity in
—which is fine—in an air of peace and freedom
as some of them have fasted or will fast or otherwise
sacrifice. A trace of movement along the frieze.

"For a symbolic hand," says this one or the other,
"lies on the pulse of protean co-Americans,
the very hand on the light table, the gong's mallet,
an instrument like my word: confusion of stillness
and motion, the *horror vacui,* and the ancient
nobility of fictive farce!" Perhaps, please,
among blot and stipple and among these nattering damned
didactic SAT and vocabulary words, which are boring
or stunning (in exigency of plot as metaphor) sometimes
to read, the poems are honored by your time and attention.

The Contemporary Poetry Series

Edited by Paul Zimmer

The Contemporary Poetry Series

Edited by Bin Ramke